# Arthur's Journey

## Written by Lorna Karras

## Illustrations: Richard Jones & Ian Winn

ISBN: 979862298301

Thank you to my husband for
rescuing Arthur and bringing
him home to us.

This book was written for my grandaughter Matilda Darcy who loves to
play with Arthur.

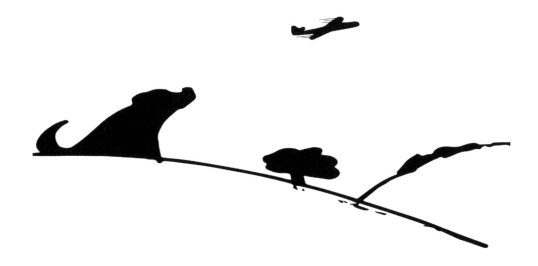

# Arthur's Journey

This book belongs to

_____

Once not so long ago on the Greek island of Samos,

Lived a young scruffy puppy called Arthur,

He had no real home,

He lived on scraps and pieces of bone.

All through the village and down to the square,

chasing and barking, searching bins where he dare,

Until….

He was caught and put on a rope

Left alone barking without any hope

Itching and scratching covered in lice.

Woo woo cried the puppy this isn't nice.

The poor little puppy was lonely and sad
Being tied to a rope was driving him mad.

With no friends to play with and nowhere to go

He snapped at flies and bees passing by

He watched the aeroplanes up in the sky,

Wishing and wishing that he could fly.

Then along came a man

Who took off his rope,

He set Arthur free.

At last he had hope.

Arthur was so happy he licked the man's face.

He ran up the street to pack his suitcase.

We must get you a passport do you have a name?

Yes my name is Arthur and

I'm very glad you came.

NAME ___Arthur___

ANIMAL ___Dog___

3452645erts 867/67686

Happy at last the puppy started to sing:

My name is  Arthur, I am a furry thing

My name is Arthur and I have a hairy chin

My name is  Arthur, I like to chase  cats

My name is  Arthur, I like to sit on laps.

My name is Manos said the man,

Let's get you a passport as soon as we can.

First you need a shower to clean your dirty coat,

Next, we'll buy a ticket and get you on a boat.

Once on the boat, rocking with the waves

**Splish splash splosh**

from the Greek island of Samos,

**Splish splash splosh**

Until……

Soon it was dark and he looked at the moon,

Thinking of all the new places to
be seen very soon.

The city of Athens was reached at first light.

The Parliament soldiers were marching;

what a wonderful sight.

Wearing red hats and guns by their side,

Arthur pulled at his lead and decided to hide.

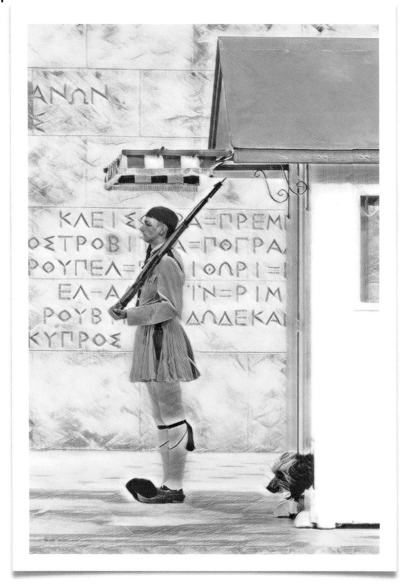

Back in the car they headed for Rome,

The city of love; could this be my new home?

"Oh no!" said the man we have further to go,

You will see some mountains covered in snow.

In Italy they stayed in Bologna in a very nice hotel,

Room service please, shall I ring the bell?

A night in Calais

And a visit to the vet,

"Ouch!" said Arthur after the final vaccination

Can we please now go for some tea and relaxation?

The following day they made their

crossing to Dover,

Where Arthur met another dog who said his

name was Rover.

Wish you were here

They jumped and chased around,

Then had some fish and chips,

Very yummy indeed said Arthur,

Licking his greasy lips.

Arthur said goodbye to his friend and

carried on his way.

Until at last the car stopped again later in the day

we're here at last Manos said handing him a bone,

The journey has been long but

we've finally reached home!

At last I feel loved and I've found a happy home,

I've travelled across Europe and

no longer need to roam,

No more searching in every single bin

now I can eat from a very shiny tin.

Now he has new friends to play with

Teddy, Hugo and Bella

Thinking to himself

I'm one very lucky fella.

Printed in Great Britain
by Amazon